hon

Marianna's Beauty Salon

Sibling Rivalry Press, LLC
PO Box 26147
Little Rock, AR 72221

info@siblingrivalrypress.com

www.siblingrivalrypress.com

ISBN: 978-1-943977-48-2

Library of Congress Control No. 2017964691

This title is housed permanently in the Rare Books and Special Collections Vault of the Library of Congress.

First Sibling Rivalry Press Edition, May 2018

Marianna's Beauty Salon

BUSHRA REHMAN

SIBLING RIVALRY PRESS
LITTLE ROCK, ARKANSAS
DISTURB / ENRAPTURE

CONTENTS

I

II

III

RAPUNZEL'S MOTHER OR A PAKISTANI WOMAN NEWLY ARRIVED IN AMERICA

With a cabbage, a box of eggs so clean she could easily forget
the source of their existence, my mother filled her silver cart
and moved in line to make her purchase.

The cashier turned a sharp glance at the small brown woman
with the pierced nose and covered head. She didn't fit
into this, an American supermarket.

"And what," asked the cashier, "are you willing to pay for this?"
She held the head of lettuce in the air. It reflected
off her rhinestone glasses and the hairspray in her hair.

"But this," said my mother, "is America. I thought there was no barter here."

"Hmmmph," said the cashier. "There's give and take all over the world.
What made you think it would be different here?"
She shook her head and her plastic hair.

"But I have money." My mother tried to act like she didn't care.
Her English broke all over her and fell apart in the air.

But the cashier cackled, "No, no, no, my dear, what I want is here."
She jabbed a nail, silver-painted and crooked, at my young mother's stomach
which I had just begun to share.

"That is the price you'll have to pay, my dear, for this fresh lettuce.
Each egg that erupts into a new-blown head will be the property
of this here supermarket, country, and nation.

"And don't even think of running because we've got the goods on you.
Along with every other immigrant, we've got your passport,
your foreign passport right here."

11

She made to reach into her too-tight jeans, but my mother, she ran out of there.
The shopping girl openly laughed behind her, and the lines and lines
of customers just stood there with their stupid grins.

My mother ran. The door opened by itself.
My mother ran, but she still found herself
in a foreign land, far away from home.

WILL HEAVEN LOOK LIKE ZEENAT AMAN?

My mother used to tape Indian movies
illegally all day long
there'd be three or four movies going
two VCRs whirring
getting all technologically horny
with the high-pitched songs
of the young female stars
the lucky ones
who got to dance with Amitabh

Their bodies would be bursting out of their saris
their lips would be all moist and warm
but untouched
and Amitabh would be there all funny
funny with his long long body
and his eyes brown and warm

My mother used to tape Indian movies
illegally all day long
there'd be three or four movies going
two VCRs whirring
their frequencies all turned on
by that subtle pre-orgasmic flurrying
that filled every love sick song

And it filled me
so that even as a child
loving and kissing
were in my dreams
and I could never quite walk
from point A to point B

But would instead jump and bounce
humming something about eyes
looking like oceans or the sea in a storm

And at night before going to sleep
I'd think about the kids
who went to kindergarten with me
and imagine all sorts of adventures
all sorts of dances and songs

But my mother, she's different now
she faces Mecca, not *Namak Halal*
and although she's still singing
verses from the Quran
it's not the same
there isn't any kind of tingling
in my feet or my gut

When I go home, I wrap my dupatta around me
my mother hugs me in-between prayers
she doesn't get off her janamaz

But I remember her being different
I remember her smiling or angry
but always something
at least something
that felt like lightning in a storm

That was her before. Now
she's like a volcano rumbling
as she sits there reading namaaz

And I wonder if when her spirit passes
when her souls starts and leaves her body
and she goes to that place she'd rather be
will Gibreel look like Amitabh
or will heaven look like Zeenat Aman?

EGGS

One time Ammi opened
up a chicken
and brought it down
to where I could see
on the kitchen floor

I was small and Ammi
had that chicken
on the ground
all cut up
so its insides showed

She was trying to teach me
something about the world

Look, she said. *Look*

That chicken was full
there were eggs, eggs, eggs
spiraling down
jammed like a string
of fake pearls

Lined up from big to small
hard marbles, soft ovals
ready to burst
with veins running
like thin rivers of blood

Ammi was trying to teach me
something about the world
I saw eggs, eggs, and more eggs
lined up, thinking they were going to grow

NASHTA

I'd wake up to the smell of pratha
and Ammi in the kitchen
making nashta for the whole family

She'd always be there by the kitchen stove
standing behind the smoke
rolling and frying the dough
and by her feet would be two
or three mice stuck in glue traps
trying to pull free

Sometimes their mouths
would be stuck
or their whiskers
I'd want to touch them
but Ammi wouldn't let me
she'd tell me to hurry
get to school, get ready

The mice would twitch and pull
until their eyes would go dull
then Ammi would throw them out

But the next morning, there'd always be more
I'd wake up to the smell of pratha
and Ammi in the kitchen
making nashta for the whole family
and the mice would be there at her feet
stuck in their glue traps
trying to pull free

OLD TELEVISION

We scattered green pellets
before we moved out
It made the mice so thirsty
they could only wander around

Drag their bodies
from corner to corner, wall to wall
but there was no way out

No holy spirit
to come down and relieve their thirst
no holy spirit
to come down and create a spring
in the cracks on the floor

I was in our new home
and couldn't hear them
their dry tongues
thin pacing

When my brother went back
he said he found them
behind the old television
their bodies shriveled
like their insides had all come out

HOME

What can I say, the garden is already buried under cement
the spiders have engrained themselves into every crack
and the ghosts of the mice glued or cut in half by the traps
have just given up on the place and walked out

What can I say, I was taken away
given a new home and told to forget

But every night, the mice
run around in my head
and every year
the crumbs
that fell
from the birthday cakes of us six children
the ones who took root
in the carpet, bloom
into full-blown cakes once again

All covered with tiny blue flames and hot pink roses
like the ones we used to gather from the garden

AMMI'S CASSETTES

The other day, I found my mother's cassettes from the Eighties
they were full of love songs from Indian movies
Ammi used to tape them from the TV
while she cleaned

And I thought back to the orange carpets
the sofas with their plastic
the way everything was dusted and perfect

I tried to fill the memory with her music
to come up with something peaceful
something splendid
but the tapes, they just didn't play that way

You see, they caught all the background noise:
the sound of babies crying
children fighting
fire engines going
and then the sound of a child being hit

The children wouldn't stop making noise
until my mother's own voice would break
then there would be nothing
but the sound of her crying
and the sound of music
in a language
my mother was dying to hear

And I thought back to the orange carpets
the way I would press my face against them
and against the plastic sofas
until the perspiration would make it stick
and listen to the sound of her crying
and all the love songs of longing

They promised everything
missing in our house
with its orange carpets
everything missing in the plastic
everything she ever recorded

SOFA BEDS

There are sofa beds growing
everywhere in Corona
on street corners, in yards

Yellow, bright orange, brown
they burst out of the ground
mushrooms come full-blown
in the middle of the night

They are elephants, birds
rhinos stopping for a moment
in the river of the street

There are sofa beds growing
everywhere in Corona
they open like night flowers
in the evening

THE OLD ITALIAN

The old Italian leans from his window
his belly hangs
over the grape vines grown like trees

When it rains we pull on them like hair
and feel the rain down our cheeks
soak our clothes, our salwar kameez

The neighborhood is no longer Italian
The old man can already see
Halal meat stores and dozens of children
playing in the streets

In the afternoons, I bring my father tea
he's always waiting at the store and smiling
his shirt covered with blood from the meat

The neighborhood is no longer Italian
The old man smokes his pipe and grieves
for days like this in the summer
when he was a child on the streets

ENOUGH

Enough! Who done this?
the old Italian belched into the evening

a circle of blood was at my feet
the train a rifle swing
over my head

to my right and left
I saw the backs of my friends
running into alleys
like mice popping
up from stove lights
their bodies close
to the counters
their hearts beating thousands
of beats per minute

Enough! Who done this?
the old Italian
cast a shadow on my forehead

above me, the kitten
had hopefully fallen asleep
her skin torn through
by the stones my friends
had killed her with

AUGUST

I remember there was a June bug
it was August
we were all on the roof
there was a silence between us
because everyone knew
I'd done something wrong
I'd have to be punished somehow
but until then
everyone was milling around
talking about the dark and the stars
but what did they know
about the dark and the stars
I just looked at the June bug
and prayed we'd
both survive
somehow

WHITE PICKET FENCE, NO

white picket fence, no, try chain link
my father so afraid of the world
he erected it, Pakistani style-ghetto style
12-foot-high fence, metal, jail, around our house
five juicy daughters to protect, one son, one wife
always pregnant, and him always at work

his best friend and him tore up the shrubbery
all around, if the white neighbors
hadn't already fled, they would have
said: *There goes the neighborhood*

increasing fear, there must have been a series
of rapes and burglaries, the greenery
couldn't hold it out, so they pulled
the bushes loose from the roots, then
laid it down, 250 feet of chain link

what did my father think, when it was all done
did he stand back from his handiwork
and drink a cup of water
did he stand back and think:
No one will hurt them now

he may have just sat down, exhausted from the effort
his small frame not meant for such heavy labor
but he could not protect us, could never protect us
he had forgotten about the snakes in the house

MARIANNA'S BEAUTY SALON

Marianna's beauty salon has become a Halal meat shop
and I wonder where all the Muslim girls will go
when they want to get their hair cut off
and feel a Dominican lady close
with all her makeup

How will all the Muslim girls get to sit
with their backs tight stiff
and the sweat in their palms
how will they sit
when they want to feel
the weight of their hair fall off

And how will the Muslim girls get to look
into sticky mirrors
to see their faces like some lost familiar
as if they were pressing themselves
down the birth canal
and paying a Dominican lady
to hold up the mirror

And after their hair's been cut
how will they get to go
with their hearts tight closed
and their faces bloodless as rocks

How will they go
to face their mothers
waiting behind kitchen walls
long braids holding them down like ropes
and in each fist a curtain rod

How will they get to cry
as the rods come down

leaving brown marks
and breaking bones
how will they cry
with their little black hairs
stuck to foreheads like traces of blood

Now when the Muslim girls go to Marianna's Beauty Salon
the Halal meat butchers will simply chop their heads off

EID AL-FITR

At night, the men climb up to the rooftops
to see if they can see the moon

The sun sets first over the beaches of Brooklyn
then the meadows of Queens

The moon appears
the small clip of a nail
a paring knife
a chalk mark
left to linger in the sky

Always the sun sets first
and like Allah's clockwork
the moon finds itself in our hands
a bird come to rest

It hangs low over buildings
crosses over street lamps
jumps rope with telephone lines
hears the Aunties' voices
through the wires
calling each other to ask:

Has anyone seen the moon yet?
Has anyone seen the moon?

MASJID

The minar and dome of our masjid
took longer to grow than trees
Our fathers bought the land, then tilled it
Before that, it was a parking lot
for the Jehovah's Witness
They sold it when the pamphlets door to door
weren't bringing in enough donations

Our fathers sowed the seeds
Qurans and janamazes. In all my years
from when I was four to sixteen
the walls went up, and then the dome grew
the same pace my breasts did

The minar too, grew to reach
the heights of the Queens sky
push up past the telephone lines
let itself poke up, respectful still
of the Episcopalian church steeple next to it
the flat brick surface of the kingdom
of the Jehovah's Witness

It was fine real estate for religion
on National street, a church
a kingdom and a masjid
crammed next to each other
wall to wall, skin to skin

And if you crossed the street
there was a Catholic store
selling crucifixes and paintings
of women and men in hell burning
The sinners looked like all of us
but I always thought that all of us
in our agony looked like Jesus

FIREHOUSE LIGHT
1995

"On fire! On fire!" the engines would wail
and the white men in shiny black boots
would stand on either side

Back then, we mis-thought them
the most handsome men alive
So different than the men in our homes
dark-bearded, all frowns and sighs
their minds preoccupied with death

But the firemen, hooo weee
speeding towards hell itself
all smiles and always waving good-bye

I remember when I left home screaming
fire in my blood, in my eyes
leaving with a white man
ah, how my parents wailed and cried
blood in the roof of the mouth
They did not wave good-bye

But how did I find myself here
on this fire escape, trapped inside
a house, a marriage, afraid to climb
I can hear the snores
I can feel the smoke between my eyes

How I wish I could open the gates
Let them rise
and rush through the streets on an engine
smiling and waving good-bye

BOOKBAG

Stolen March 14

Some people say it's dumb to get attached to things
but you know sometimes you really can't help it
when you've got a thing, and so many times
it's been the only thing you've got.

When you can turn to it and say,
"It's just you and me kid," and then laugh a lot.

You know you're never really alone
when you've got a thing you can carry around,
when the thing itself carries your toothbrush, your socks
because you never know where you're going to end up.

I mean what are you supposed to do?
How can you not get attached
when it's the only thing that's taught you the lesson
of what was essential and what was not.

You say, "I don't need anyone now.
I've got my things, you don't know how
or where I'm going, and you can't come along
but my bookbag can."

I mean what are you supposed to do?
How can you not get attached when there's always a diary handy,
condoms, pencils and pens, scraps of addresses of people
to whom you never give a thought?

Of course you're always pulling the scraps up
every time you're trying to get change for cigarettes or the bus
or the toll-free number of your advisor in New York,
but mostly change, the condoms just dust and rot.

I mean maybe my bookbag heard me
the day I was in David's garden
and said, "I'm going to stop moving around.
I don't care about having adventures anymore.
I just want a home and a garden
and I'm so tired I don't even care
if it sounds like a magazine."

I said no more traveling
and I know my bookbag heard me.
Why else would it have disappeared?

Somehow though it's been happening lately.
My jeans wore out, my boots hurt when I walk.
And I called long distance yesterday to mourn the loss,
all of us old friends separated and falling off
Anti-depressants, Valium and marriage.

"Is it such a sin to be lonely?" one asked.
"It is," I said. "It is."

I called them all. You know how it is.
Some people say it's dumb to get attached to things
but you know, sometimes you really can't help it
when you've got a thing and so many times
it's been the only thing you've got.

BRIAN'S SILVER DOLLARS

I'm thinking of how I've never had to use Brian's silver dollars
the ones he gave me in Massachusetts before I left, saying:

My grandfather gave these to me when I was a kid
He said they'd be worth a lot someday
and to keep them, but I want you to have them
Now if you keep them, you'll always have money

We both laughed because we knew
I'd always be a thin sliver away from gutter poor
I'd always be ill-clothed, hungry
moving from place to place, not keeping
a lover, a job, an apartment, a space
never having more than spare change in my pockets
or anything to eat
but flying flying all the time
flying by the sheer will of my movements

And I'm thinking of the two years since the last time I saw him
on the drive when he was going to Virginia
and I caught a bus to California from New York
and we had sex on the way one last time in the truck
it was never sad, our coming together our going apart

Yet some of my sweetest memories of a man
are with him, how he used to take baths with me
how we used to make barbecued chicken and chili in huge pots
and eat it for over a week, and how we lived
all summer off a jar of quarters

(that was the most sweet)

In the two years since then
I've gone without a home
I've gotten on my hands and knees

for pennies on the floor
I've asked complete strangers for money

(and gotten $500 from the first)

I've held up lines at the metro north station, at the port authority
counting out pennies and nickels and dimes

(knowing full well people would kill me
if they knew I had two silver dollars in my pockets)

My grandfather gave these to me when I was a kid
He said they'd be worth a lot someday
and to keep them, but I want you to have them
Now if you keep them, you'll always have money

Just this morning I spent two hours
looking for change to buy a subway token
I found my old battered wallet
inside were Brian's silver dollars
next to a Bank of New York card
for an account in which I only had a penny

(one I had to cancel soon or they were going to charge me money)

I looked around the apartment again and this time
I found change a male guest had left behind
I figured I'd take it for rent

Brian's silver dollars were saved once again

The funny thing was there were three silver dollars in the wallet
I guess somewhere along the way I've acquired a third one
I don't know which one is which, so I keep all three
not wanting to lose the two I originally got

So now I have three silver dollars
I guess that's what people call savings

OVARY

I left my ovary on the subway last night.
Stepped out. Felt light.
Heard the doors close behind me,
then realized I'd left my ovary behind.

If there was an honest person left
in New York, maybe they'd return it.
But you can get 2000 dollars for an egg,
at least that's what the *Village Voice* says.
And with enough eggs in there
to last me a lifetime, whoever found it
is going to be rich.

I reported my ovary lost the next day.
The woman who answered the phone
said, "We've got lots of hearts,
livers, kidneys, and brains,
but no ovary."

"No ovary? I asked. "Please,
would you look again?"

She sighed, but then being a woman
I guess she did understand.
"What did they look like?"

"Like walnuts, kind of shriveled and red."

"Contents?"

"All my unborn children,
my mother's smile and my father's laugh,
my sister's tongue and my crooked teeth,
but also the potential for genius . . ."

There was a pause on the other end
then she said, "I'll be right back."

When she returned, she said
there was nothing like my ovary
but that I should call again.

I called the next morning.

"You? Well, today
I have one limb, and one liver
in pretty bad condition."

"Anything else?"

"A handful of fetuses like a bucketful of shrimp."

"Anything else?"

"A human head."

"Is it Leary's?"

"Yes, he's dead. But I've got a long braid of hair,
a couple of kneecaps, a stomach that's full, but
quickly becoming empty. But no ovary,
no ovary," she said.

If there was an honest person left
in New York, maybe they'd return it.
But you can get 2000 dollars for an egg,
at least that's what the *Village Voice* says.

But still I call every morning
and it's always the same woman.
She tells me about all the pieces
of people she finds missing
and I tell her about
all the pieces of me I've lost
and not found yet.

WORRY AND ANXIETY HAVE WORN ME DOWN TO THE BONE

there was no rug on the floor
and the old lady from downstairs
would crawl up on her hands through the wood
and show up at the door, screaming

there was no rug on the floor
and any scrape or movement
would start the beating up
from down below
the wooden broom, gunfire
and the lady would crawl
then show up at the door, screaming

there was no rug on my floor
and every time I stepped
every move from me, the creak of the bed
would unleash the stream as if she was
a puppet tied to the hooks in the wall

every move I'd make would send
an electric force, fire through her body
the screaming of her would red the electric
until she'd run up the stairs, not content
to bang on our floor, her ceiling,
she'd try to break down our iron door

bang! bang! bang!

I can hear you, she'd say, you cockroaches
you whores, I can hear you breathing
breathin' on the door

I couldn't bring myself to look at her
so I closed my eyes and imagined

her apartment full of upholstered chairs
imagined the soiled lampshades, lamps
the bible with all the names missing

she'd have to stand on a chair
with a broom in her hand
pushing up against the ceiling

bang! bang! bang!

outside, police rounded up boys on the street
outside, garbage filled the knots in the trees
outside, pigeons lived and died dirty

BEFORE I LEFT NEW YORK

Before I left New York
the sky was unzippering itself everyday
like a dirty old man on the train

The rain splattered
hit down and popped
before I left New York

There was darkness
every morning I woke up
laundry left hanging
wet t-shirts with no skin

Outside my sister's window
the vines grew tight as knots
waterbugs crawled up drains
and chased us down the parquet

All the passing day, the streets
filled up, umbrellas sprung
from cracks in the sidewalk
the sky was trying to drown us
the wrong way up
before I left New York

SOMETIMES I WONDER

Sometimes I wonder what it was
if it was all those Long Island Iced Teas we drank
or the way we sat so close on the bed
or the way she said the things she said:

I was only seven years old
he called me into the room
he told me to get down
and he stuck my head between his legs
I was crying and spitting
but he wouldn't stop
he told me he'd kill me
if I ever told

And maybe it was because
I knew him
the half-crippled body
the completely decayed mind
the way he tore her family apart
again and again

The way he'd steal checkbooks
forge signatures
until her mother's checks would bounce
the way the stink of his sweat
would come up from the basement
and beat through the house

And maybe it was because I loved her
that I cried so much and so hard
it brought even her to stop
and begin to kiss me
or was it me who began to kiss her
but we kissed and we kissed
until the crying stopped

THE DIFFERENCE

It's the difference between
whether you talk to the girl or not
whether you carry the moon home
in the seat of your pants
burning and cool
ready to lay it on your tongue
in the privacy of your room
and let its holy light burn through
your blood
Or whether you walk home
with the moon in your stomach
heavy as a rock
with all the sidewalks pulling you down
and all the well-lit buildings
of a midtown night winking on and off
saying we know you, you're the one who
goes home alone and types in the dark
with the small cut of your window
always blocking the light of the moon off

ASLEEP

She is asleep, and I am full
of longing in the kitchen
Having finished the toast, I place
the wet spoon on the crumb-covered plate
Having sipped from the cup I watch
the butter melt in the air

The sun, it comes through
and draws a clear white band
across the checkered linoleum

YOU SAY YOU MISS MY HAIR

For bald girls everywhere

don't you see
now the entire night
and the light are my hair

that the fences on delancey street
the old columns
the broken figures and statues
now these are my hair

(your soft hands on my head are my hair)

the broken english of a mother
running across the street
the newsstands
the mailboxes
the telephone lines
they're all getting
caught up in my hair

and all of brooklyn bridge behind me
the twin towers, the hot pink top
of the empire state building, the water
turning from blue to black, the tiny
green point of the statue of liberty
have all become my hair

all the streets
and what I feel for you
are my hair

see, if you touch me again
you'll feel the whole world
run through your fingers

OYSTERS

I'm all torn up by oysters
and the scars friends bring
strange things happen
in automobiles heading to
and from Florida

There are secret maps
that should remain locked
in the glove box

Because once unfolded
our stories and thoughts
will not fold into themselves again
and we will become blind women
driving across Florida, that burning land

GEESE

Why did I choose to call her then
and allow her to spit in my mouth

When only moments before
I'd been humming in the kitchen
dark storm moving across Brooklyn
clouds pulling themselves
over open fields of apartments

When only moments before
a flock of geese
far away enough out
to be specks, motes in the sky
had flapped in a straying line
every goose for himself

When with a cold slap, I'd felt their bodies
heavy and fat, I'd felt their cold
wind had pushed against my chest
the sky had become suddenly thunderous
clouds had tucked themselves
into the sides of apartments

Why did I choose to call her then
when only moments before
I'd seen a thin line of geese
thread itself against the sky

YOUR LOCK

Your lock is more delightful to me than a hundred keys.

– Jalal al-Din Rumi

It is the missing clasp of your body
that shudders me awake
and before I fall asleep
I replay all the tightly
wound metal
of our kisses, all
the ways our bodies
resisted, all
the ways we
came unhinged
let a thousand doors
fall from their
places, a thousand
bees fly from
their nests

AT THE MUSEUM OF NATURAL HISTORY

Love is a tyrannous prince.

— Jalal al-Din Rumi

As we both look up at the Tyrannosaurus Rex
its bones painted black, its danger extinct
I can hear the sounds of children
echo throughout the museum

And we are not afraid this way
to stand a few inches away from each other
we are not afraid because it's over
the Tyrannosaurus Rex does not scare us
we don't scare each other

It's over
the bones are beginning to fade
and bleach in our failure

But if one day someone finds our bones
and decides to lay them right next to each other
will they lay them in their proper ways
will they mix up my hip with yours
will they place the fingers of my hands
on someone else's palms

Will they ever know
this flesh answered the other
that my fingers traveled all over
the empty space around your bones

OUR NATURAL HISTORY

We spend hours
in the ocean life section
watching all the real and fake fish
swim silently or light up
with bioluminescence
when they are in the mood
to kick it with a passing fish

We watch while the mollusks
let the weight of the water carry their shells
watch while the giant whales flow up ahead
letting their whole bodies
float in the wild air

I watch you
move through
the dark hallway
you are perfect, fluid
your eyes near-sighted
your fingernails clipped

And it seems so strange to me
that while the whales were swimming
and pulling their bulk and length across the sea floor
while the jellyfish and worms were being made
you and I were tearing each other to pieces
you and I were so afraid

But these are the things to fear:
the crabs with their giant claws, the sharks
the beasts who don't know their own strength
who could swallow us with a yawn
and then swim away

I watch you move through the dark hallway
and can't believe we were up here on dry land
with nothing but a little water in the air
that we walked sluggishly with fear
while all the fish and whales
danced downstairs

WHAT DO YOU DO WHEN YOUR LOVER IS IN BED WITH ANOTHER MAN?

I become the dinosaur wind
I wander the earth lonely and fierce
burning in the sun's radiance

I become the tornado wind
an emptiness that flies over houses
indecent in my choices
of who I keep, who I spare

I become the elephant wind
and bury all the bones of my family

I become the pilgrim wind
the minnow wind, the stray dog wind
I growl and chase kids down the street
I become the rocking horse wind
girls ride me to their dreams

DID SPRING NEVER DECEIVE YOU
WITH KISSES THAT DIDN'T BLOSSOM?

Yes, as a matter of fact it did, just this spring,
when pink was all the rage in Brooklyn,
and storekeepers hired young boys to sweep flowers
from their doorsteps. When air was heavy
and people walked around drugged,
when pharmaceutical companies tried desperately
to prevent love, spring did deceive me.

Yes, it did, while his body lay across my bed,
cherry trees dropped flowers like winks from taxi cabs.
Thin white petals and hard rose peeling fell into my skin,
and the whole world felt new again. There was a window
and pink blossoms, a tree that swung up and knocked quietly,
other times left us to rest.

But while a riot of blossoms turned the streets of Brooklyn
into something beautiful, something foreign,
while the 99-cent store owners, the ones who had wandered
too far from Atlantic, swept their doorsteps, he left,
and I lay on my bed and watched the flowers fall,
the tiny green leaves uncurl and grow into plain green leaves,
just as I knew they would.

Yes, spring did deceive me, his body, the tree, the window,
pink, Brooklyn, and all the rage.

PHONE CALL BOMBS

There are phone call bombs
that blow up
whenever we talk these days

I can hear them ticking
when I innocently call you
and when you answer the fuse is lit

B-BOY

I say, I always want you to be that man
standing on your head, trying to impress me
with your b-boy antics
an era I lived through
but was never allowed to experience

We might as well be in the schoolyard
and the trees and the homes around us
could just fall off, leave behind:
pavement, fences,
and screams of kids,
screaming and then, you
among the boys, me
among the girls, you
not looking my way,
but with all my body, I know
your awareness is focused on me,
and you know, even though
I look away, stand quiet,
there is already a fluttering
underneath my skirt,
my hair rises up
just a little in the wind,
as you throw your body down,
raise yourself up, your body strong, tense

Everyone is smiling, and I am smiling with everyone else,
but I know, and you know, that headspin is for me

THE CAR

As the car slows to a stop
the darkness wells around us
we are on the edge
all is quiet

it's been a month
of everything falling apart

we make our way home
in the pitch black
do not talk

I draw myself a bath
think of my parents
how little money they had
how little money we have now

one day this era
will be called a Depression
but tonight
we beat ourselves against the walls
for being so broke
for the car we must leave
on the side of the road

easy enough to forget
we are being sucked dry by vultures
easy enough to forget
there is a war

but quiet now
lay down beside him
forget, turn on the 70s soul
love him on the bed, still
in your towel, let it all ease out

Forget there is not enough money
not enough money to pay the rent in the house

I LOVE YOU/PERVERT

I start to feel like a pervert
when I think of how many times
I've watched you sleep

our schedules mismatched
so that when the thin slim outline
of our falling comes together
we sigh and rub
make fissures and fractures
allow the chairs to stand in the rain
forget to pay the bills
water the plants

but your sleeping body is soft
is my comfort in the morning
and night. You've taken the place
of all the books and papers
that filled my bed before
now there is heaviness,
there is your weight,
there is your body,
always sleeping

ENCYCLOPEDIA OF THE SOLAR SYSTEM

in perpetual darkness
Pluto is farthest from the Sun

when I construct a rough map of light
dark areas on both our bodies
I think of this

my thoughts two tiny moons orbiting

METEORS

to sleep all day in loving arms
or call my mother and hear her say
Bushra? I was thinking of you right now

to sleep all day in loving arms
or spend the morning
feeling the sun warm the linoleum
looking out the window and thinking:

I am dealing with nature
when I'm dealing with the weather
I'm not really missing out
I still get to see the moon
with its many shades
and its many shapes
I still get to see the sun
and have it light me up
all stars and warm

but maybe I'm lucky
because I've been to the country
and seen the suns burn out
and shoot across the dark

(and how many suns there are)

they say ours will too
and I believe it
because haven't I seen them fall
some real fast, some real slow
stars, meteors and fireballs

until it seemed everything
was either stars or space or the light in between us
until it seemed even she and me
were only a tiny part

but that love was the light that moved between us
that would move on without us
that would always shoot
across the dark

ACKNOWLEDGMENTS

Acknowledgments are made to the following publications in which some of the poems, at times in earlier versions, first appeared.

"Ammi's Cassettes" appeared in *Mizna: Prose, Poetry, and Art Exploring Arab America* (Winter 2004).

"Bookbag" appeared in *SALT* (Winter 2002).

"Rapunzel's Mother or a Pakistani Woman Newly Arrived in America" appeared in *Mizna: Prose, Poetry, and Art Exploring Arab America* (Winter 2004).

"Sometimes I Wonder" and "You Say You Miss My Hair" appeared in *Queering Sexual Violence: Radical Voices from Within the Anti-Violence Movement* (Jennifer Patterson, editor; Riverdale Avenue Books/A Magnus Imprint/2016).

"Will Heaven look like Zeenat Aman?" appeared in *SAMAR: South Asian Magazine of Action and Reflection* (December 2001) and in *Asian American Literary Review* (September 2011).

NOTES

"Did Spring Never Deceive You With Kisses That Didn't Blossom?"
  The title is a question from Pablo Neruda's *The Book of Questions*.
  Translated by William O'Daly. Copper Canyon Press, 2001.

"Eid al-Fitr"
  A Muslim holiday whose date is based on the sighting of the
  crescent moon.

"Rapunzel's Mother or a Pakistani Woman Newly Arrived in America"
  When Rapunzel's mother was pregnant, she developed a craving
  for vegetables from the witch's garden. When Rapunzel's father
  tried to steal them, he was caught and so terrified, he agreed to give
  the witch his firstborn child, Rapunzel.

"Will Heaven look like Zeenat Aman?"
  Zeenat Aman is a legendary Bollywood actress; Amitabh Bachchan
  is a legendary Bollywood actor; *Namak Halal* is a movie starring
  Amitabh Bachchan. If you don't recognize these names, just insert
  the latest Bollywood superstars.

"Your Lock" and "At the Museum of Natural History"
  Quotes from Jalal al-Din Rumi are from *Mystical Poems of Rumi 1:
  First Selection, Poems 1-200*. Translated by A.J. Arberry. University
  of Chicago Press, 1968.

THANK YOUS

These poems were written over a period of twenty years, so my gratitude is endless, but here goes: Thank you to the all the artists and activists in the early collectives of SAWCC and SALGA who helped me know there was a place for this poetry in the world. Thank you to Bryan Borland, Seth Pennington, and Sibling Rivalry Press for believing.

Thank you to Ben Perowsky, Sa'dia Rehman, Andrea Dobrich, Anastacia Holt, Adele Swank, Adeeba Rana, Aracelis Girmay, Bao Phi, Cathy Linh Che, Chamindika Wanduragala, Chitra Ganesh, Daisy Hernández, Diedra Barber, Holly Blake, Ishle Yi Park, Jaishri Abichandani, Joseph O. Legaspi, Kamilah Aisha Moon, Nina Sharma, Rekha Malhotra, Saba Waheed, Sally Lee, Samantha Thornhill, Sarita Khurana, Soniya Munshi, Stas Gibbs, Tazeen Khan, Yvette Ho, and all my Two Truths friends for all the love and support over the years.

Special thanks to the Asian American Writers' Workshop, Barbara Deming Memorial Foundation, Cave Canem, City Lore, Cullman Center for Teachers, Headlands Center for the Arts, Hedgebrook, Jerome Foundation, Kundiman, Norcroft, Saltonstall, South Asian Lesbian and Gay Association, South Asian Women's Creative Collective, Soul Mountain Retreat, and the Vermont Studio Center.

ABOUT THE AUTHOR

Bushra Rehman grew up in Corona, Queens, but her mother says she was born in an ambulance flying through the streets of Brooklyn. This would explain a few things. Bushra was a vagabond poet who traveled for years with nothing more than a Greyhound ticket and a book bag full of poems.

Her first novel *Corona*, a dark comedy about being South Asian American, was noted by *Poets & Writers* among 2013's Best Debut Fiction and featured in *LA Review of Books* as a work of notable South-Asian American Literature. She co-edited the anthology *Colonize This! Young Women of Color on Today's Feminism*, one of *Ms. Magazine*'s "100 Best Non-Fiction Books of All Time." Her next novel, *Corona: Stories of a Queens Girlhood*, is forthcoming from Tor/Macmillan.

Marianna's Beauty Salon is Bushra's first collection of poetry.

ABOUT THE PRESS

Sibling Rivalry Press is an independent press based in Little Rock, Arkansas. It is a sponsored project of Fractured Atlas, a nonprofit arts service organization. Contributions to support the operations of Sibling Rivalry Press are tax-deductible to the extent permitted by law, and your donations will directly assist in the publication of work that disturbs and enraptures. To contribute to the publication of more books like this one, please visit our website and click *donate*.

Sibling Rivalry Press gratefully acknowledges the following donors, without whom this book would not be possible:

Liz Ahl

Stephanie Anderson

Priscilla Atkins

John Bateman

Sally Bellerose & Cynthia Suopis

Jen Benka

Dustin Brookshire

Sarah Browning

Russell Bunge

Michelle Castleberry

Don Cellini

Philip F. Clark

Risa Denenberg

Alex Gildzen

J. Andrew Goodman

Sara Gregory

Karen Hayes

Wayne B. Johnson & Marcos L. Martínez

Jessica Manack

Alicia Mountain

Rob Jacques

Nahal Suzanne Jamir

Bill La Civita

Mollie Lacy

Anthony Lioi

Catherine Lundoff

Adrian M.

Ed Madden

Open Mouth Reading Series

Red Hen Press

Steven Reigns

Paul Romero

Erik Schuckers

Alana Smoot

Stillhouse Press

KMA Sullivan

Billie Swift

Tony Taylor

Hugh Tipping

Eric Tran

Ursus Americanus Press

Julie Marie Wade

Ray Warman & Dan Kiser

Anonymous (14)

Lightning Source UK Ltd.
Milton Keynes UK
UKHW01f0747230518
323075UK00001B/222/P